New Testament

Timeless Bible Stories

Illustrated by Kelly Pulley

NEW TESTAMENT

NEW TESTAMENT

An Angel Visits Mary

Luke 1:26–38

God sent the *angel* Gabriel to visit
a young woman. Her name was Mary.
She was scared. She had never seen
an angel before.

Gabriel said, "Don't be afraid. You are very special to God. You will become pregnant and give birth to a son.
You must name him Jesus.
He will be called the Son of the Most High God."

Mary asked, "How can it be so?
I am not married."

Gabriel answered, "With God,
all things are possible."

Mary said, "I love God. I will do
what he has chosen me to do."

Baby Jesus Is Born

Luke 2:1–7

Mary loved Joseph. Mary and Joseph
were going to be married soon.
Joseph lived in Nazareth, but his
family lived in Bethlehem.

A new leader named Caesar ordered all
people to go back to their homeland.
He wanted to count all the people
in his kingdom. So Mary and Joseph
went to Bethlehem.

Mary was going to have her baby soon.
When they arrived in Bethlehem,
they looked for a safe place to sleep,
but all the inns were full.

Finally, a man was able to help them.
He said, "I do not have any rooms left,
but you are welcome to sleep
in the stable."

Joseph made a warm place for Mary
to rest. While they were there,
little baby Jesus was born.

Mary wrapped Jesus in strips of cloth
and gently laid him in a *manger*.

Shepherds Visit

Luke 2:8–20

On the night Jesus was born,
shepherds were watching their sheep.
Suddenly, an angel stood before them,
and God's light shined all around.

The angel said, "Do not be afraid. I bring joyful news to all people. Today, in the town of Bethlehem, a *Savior* has been born! He is lying in a manger."

Then a choir of angels appeared.
They sang, "Glory to God in the highest!
Peace and goodwill to everyone on earth!"

The shepherds rushed to Bethlehem.
There they found baby Jesus.
They told Mary and Joseph
what the angel said.

20

As they returned to their sheep,
the shepherds told everyone what they
had seen and heard. All along the way,
the shepherds shouted praises to God.

Simeon and Anna
Meet Baby Jesus

Luke 2:25–38

Mary and Joseph took baby Jesus
to the *temple*. There they met
a godly man named Simeon.

Simeon took Jesus in his arms and praised God. He knew Jesus was the Savior of all people. Then Simeon blessed Jesus, Mary, and Joseph.

A prophet named Anna lived at the
temple. She prayed to God every day.

When Anna saw baby Jesus,
she thanked God. She told everyone
in the temple, "This is God's Son,
the Savior of the world!"

The Bright Star and Three Visitors

Matthew 2:1–12

When Jesus was born, God put a special
star in the sky. Some Wise Men who
lived far away saw this star.
They knew it was a sign from God
that a new king had been born.

The Wise Men followed the star.
On their way, they stopped in the city
of Jerusalem to see King Herod.
The Wise Men wanted to ask him
about the baby king.

Now, Herod was a mean king.
He tried to trick the Wise Men.
"You must find him for me so
I can worship him, too," he said.

The star led the Wise Men to Bethlehem.
There they found little Jesus.
They worshiped him and gave him
gifts fit for a king: gold and
sweet-smelling spices.

An angel appeared to the Wise Men
in a dream. He warned them,
"Do not go back to King Herod."
So the Wise Men went home on
a different road.

An Angry King

Matthew 2:13–23

When the Wise Men did not return,
King Herod became very angry.

He yelled at his soldiers,
"Go and find the boy!
I will be the *only* king of the Jews!"

But God's angel warned Joseph
in a dream, "Take your family and
escape to Egypt. Do not return
until I tell you it is safe."

That night, Joseph and Mary left
for Egypt with baby Jesus.

Years later, God's angel said to Joseph
in a dream, "King Herod is dead.
Now, it is safe to leave Egypt."
So Joseph, Mary, and Jesus left Egypt
and went back home to Nazareth.

Jesus Is Lost!

Luke 2:41–52

Jesus grew up in Nazareth. Every year,
Jesus and his family would go to
Jerusalem to celebrate the *Passover* Feast.

When Jesus was twelve, they went
to the Feast as usual. The streets
were crowded with people.

On the way back home to Nazareth,
Mary and Joseph couldn't find Jesus.
They asked their relatives and friends,
"Have you seen Jesus?"
But no one knew where he was.

Mary and Joseph went back to Jerusalem.
They looked and looked for Jesus.

Finally, after three days, they found him!
Jesus was talking with the teachers
in the temple. The teachers were amazed.
Jesus was very wise for such a young boy.

Mary and Joseph rushed to Jesus. "We were so worried about you!" said Mary.

Jesus knew God was his Father. He said,
"I had to come to my Father's house."
He loved and obeyed his parents, too.
So he returned home with them
and grew stronger and wiser.

John Baptizes Jesus

Matthew 3:1–17; Mark 1:1–11; Luke 3:1–22; John 1:1–34

John was born just before Jesus was.
They were cousins. When John
grew up, he lived in the desert
and ate bugs and honey.

John told the people about God.
They asked him many questions about
what is right and what is wrong.
John told them to be good and
kind and honest.

John preached about God's forgiveness.
Many people decided to follow God.
John *baptized* the people in a river.

John told the people to get ready for a
special person who would save them from
their sins. One day Jesus came to the river.
John knew Jesus was that special person.
Jesus told him, "I need to be baptized
by you." John was surprised, but Jesus
said, "It is right for you to do this."

So John took Jesus into the Jordan River
and baptized him. The *Holy Spirit* came
down from heaven in the form of a dove.
It landed on Jesus. Jesus smiled.
Then God said, "This is my Son, and
I love him. I am very pleased with him."

Jesus Chooses His Disciples

Matthew 4:18–22; 9:9; 10:1–4; Mark 1–3; Luke 5–6

Jesus began to tell people about God.
He knew he had a lot of work to do,
and he went to find some helpers.

As Jesus was walking along the seashore,
he saw some fishermen.
Jesus called to them, "Come. Follow me.
I will make you fishers of *people*."

Right away, they left their boats
and followed Jesus. Their names were
Peter, Andrew, James, and John.

Later, Jesus met a tax collector named
Matthew. His job was to get the tax money
from the people and give it to the king.
Matthew quit his job to follow Jesus, too.

Jesus chose some more people.
Their names were Philip, Bartholomew,
Thomas, and another man named James.

JOHN

JAMES
SON OF ZEBEDEE

PETER

MATTHEW

ANDREW

Thaddaeus, Simon, and Judas joined them,
too. Jesus now had twelve new followers.
He called them his *disciples*.
Jesus taught them about God's love.

Jesus' First Miracle

John 2:1–11

Jesus went to a wedding with his mother
Mary and his disciples.

Mary heard the servants say,
"There is no more wine.
What can we do?"
Mary told the servants,
"Do what Jesus tells you to do."

Jesus said, "Fill up six jars of water.
Dip out a cup and give it to your master."

When they did, they saw wine instead
of water! The servants were amazed.
When their master tasted the wine,
he told the groom, "You have saved
the very best wine for last!"
The disciples were also amazed.
This was Jesus' first *miracle*.

Jesus Teaches on a Mountain

Matthew 5:1–12; 6:25–34; Luke 6:17–23; 12:22–31

All sorts of people went to see Jesus.
Children, mothers, fathers,
grandmas, and grandpas.
They all wanted to hear what
he was teaching.

"Look at the birds," said Jesus.
"Do they store up food in a barn?
No. God feeds them."

"Look at the flowers," said Jesus.
"They don't work or make clothes.
God dresses them in lush leaves
and pretty petals."

Then Jesus said, "You are much more important than birds. You are much more important than flowers.
So do not worry. If God takes care of them, God will take care of you."

The Lord's Prayer

Matthew 6:9–13; Luke 11:1–4 (NIV)

When Jesus was on the mountain,
he taught the people how to pray.
Jesus said,

"Our Father in heaven,
hallowed be your name,
your kingdom come,
your will be done
on earth as it is in heaven.
Give us today our daily bread.
Forgive us our debts,
as we also have forgiven our debtors.
And lead us not into temptation,
but deliver us from the evil one."

Amen.

A Captain's Faith

Matthew 8:5–13

Jesus came down the mountain
to a nearby city.
Crowds of people gathered to see him.

An army captain said, "Lord Jesus,
my servant is very sick. Please,
will you help him?" Jesus said,
"I will go to your house and heal him."

The captain replied, "You do not need
to go to my house. Just say the word
and my servant will be healed."

Jesus was amazed. "I have not found
anyone whose *faith* is so strong," he said.
Then Jesus said to the captain, "Go!
Your servant is healed."
The captain ran home. He was happy
to see his servant well again!

A Hole in the Roof

Matthew 9:1–8; Mark 2:1–12; Luke 5:17–26

Jesus was at a house preaching.
Many people gathered there because
they heard he was healing the sick.

The house was overflowing with people.
Many had to stand outside. There was no
room left, not even outside the door.

Down the road lived a man who
could not walk. He was paralyzed.
His friends believed Jesus could heal him.

They carried him to the house.
It was still too crowded.
So they carried him up to the roof.

The man's friends made a hole and
lowered him down to Jesus.
Jesus saw that the men had faith.
He knew how much they loved
their friend.

Jesus said to the man,
"Your sins are forgiven."
The man stood up and walked!
The crowd praised God.

Jesus Calms the Storm

Matthew 8:23–27

Jesus and his disciples got into a boat.
They wanted to cross the sea.

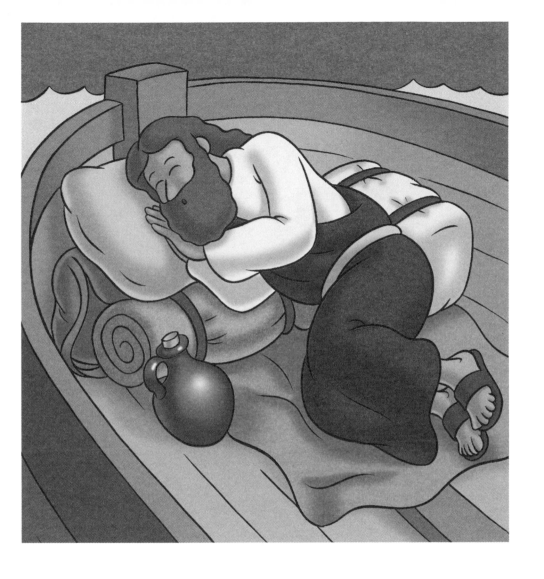

Jesus took a nap.
The waves gently rocked
the boat back and forth.

75

Suddenly a great storm came up.
Waves splashed over the boat.
Winds whipped around the disciples.

They woke Jesus up and shouted,
"The boat is sinking! Don't you care?"

Jesus asked, "Why are you so afraid?
Don't you have any faith at all?"
Then Jesus told the storm to stop.
Right away it was calm.

The disciples were amazed. They said
to each other, "Who is this man Jesus?
Even the wind and the waves obey him!"

Two Miracles

Matthew 9:18–26; Mark 5:21–43; Luke 8:40–56

One day, a man named Jairus came to
see Jesus. He cried, "Jesus! Please come
heal my daughter. She is dying."

"If you would just touch my daughter,"
Jairus said, "she would be healed." So
Jesus and his disciples went with Jairus.

A large crowd followed Jesus
as he walked to Jairus's house.

Just then, a woman pushed through
the crowd toward Jesus. She had been
sick for twelve years. The doctors
could not heal her.

The woman believed that Jesus could heal her. She thought, *I know if I just touch his clothes, I will be healed.*

As the woman got closer to Jesus,
she reached out and touched him.
She was healed at that moment!
Jesus stopped and turned around.

"Who touched me?" Jesus asked.
"I felt power go out of me."
The woman knelt before Jesus and said,
"I am the one who touched you."
Jesus said, "Your faith has made
you well. Go in peace."

Finally Jesus arrived at Jairus's house.
The people said it was too late.
His daughter had already died.

Jesus said, "Jairus, trust me.
Your daughter is not dead.
She is sleeping."

Jesus told everyone to leave the house.
Then Jairus and his wife went with Jesus
into the girl's bedroom. Jesus knelt down
beside her and said, "Wake up, my child."

Right away she opened her eyes and
climbed out of bed! Jairus and his wife
were overcome with joy.

A Fishermen's Net

Matthew 13:47–49

Jesus told a story. "One day," he said,
"some fishermen took their boat out."

"They threw their net into the water.
All kinds of fish swam in the lake."

"When the fishermen returned to shore,
they dragged their net out of the water
and looked through their catch," said Jesus.

"They kept all the good fish and tossed out all the bad fish." Jesus said, "The fishermen's net is like God's *kingdom*."

"Everyone wants to be part of his kingdom. But the angels will come and separate the godly people from the ungodly people."

"The godly people will live in heaven
with me forever."

Jesus Feeds Thousands

Matthew 14:13–22; Mark 6:30–44; Luke 9:10–17; John 6:1–15

Jesus and his disciples were tired.
They needed a quiet place to rest.
So they got into a boat and pushed off
from shore. A crowd followed the boat.

Over 5,000 people had come to see
Jesus. Even though he was tired,
Jesus wanted to help them. He
climbed out of the boat, and he
began to bless and heal many people.

Later that day, the disciples said to Jesus,
"It is getting late. These people should
go home and eat dinner."

Jesus replied, "We can feed them.
See if anyone has any food to share."

The disciples found one boy. He had
five loaves of bread and two small fish.
Jesus said, "Bring the boy to me."

The disciples asked, "How will so little food feed this many people?"
Jesus said, "You will see. Have the people sit down." Then Jesus took the bread and gave thanks to God.

His disciples gave bread and fish
to everyone. To their surprise,
twelve baskets were left over!

Jesus Walks on Water

Matthew 14:22–33; Mark 6:45–51; John 6:15–20

Jesus told his disciples to go
on ahead of him.

Then Jesus walked up a mountainside
to pray. Storm clouds filled the sky.
Jesus could see the disciples in the boat.
They were having trouble.

The wind swooshed. The waves sloshed.
The boat was tossed about.

Suddenly, the disciples saw someone
walking on the water toward them.
They thought it was a ghost!

Jesus called out to them,
"It is I. Do not be afraid!"
The disciples still weren't sure.
Peter said, "If you really are Jesus,
let me walk out to you."
Jesus replied, "Come!"

Peter stepped out of the boat. He began
walking on the water toward Jesus. Then
Peter looked at the wind and the waves.
He became afraid. Suddenly he started
to sink. "Lord, save me!" Peter cried out.
Jesus reached out and pulled Peter up.

"Why didn't you trust me?" Jesus asked
Peter. They climbed into the boat and
the storm stopped. The disciples
worshiped Jesus. They said,
"Truly you are the son of God!"

Jesus Heals a Blind Beggar

John 9:1–12

Jesus and his disciples saw a blind beggar.
He had been blind since he was born.
The disciples asked Jesus, "Teacher,
did this man sin? Or did his parents?
Is that why he is blind?"

"No one sinned," said Jesus. "This
happened so that God's work could be
shown in his life." Then Jesus spit on
the ground and made mud out of it
with his hands. He gently spread
the mud on the blind man's eyes.

Then Jesus told the man,
"Go to the Pool of Siloam
and wash off the mud."

As soon as the mud was washed off, the
man could see! Everyone was amazed.
They wanted to find out more about Jesus.

Money in a Fish

Matthew 17:24–27

It was time to pay the temple tax.
This money was used to fix up the temple.

One day, some tax collectors said to Peter,
"Jesus does not pay the temple tax, does
he?" Peter replied, "Of course he does."

Before Peter could ask Jesus what to do,
Jesus told him, "Even though I am the
Son of God, I will pay the tax. Go fishing.
Take the first fish you catch. Look in its
mouth and you will find a coin.
Take it and give it to the tax collectors.
It will pay my tax and yours."

Peter caught a fish. He opened its
mouth and found a coin inside!
It was exactly enough to pay
the tax collectors.

The Good Samaritan

Luke 10:25–37

One day, a lawyer put Jesus to the test.
He said, "I know the law says to love God
with all my heart and to love my neighbor
as myself. But who is my neighbor?"

Jesus told him this *parable*:
"A man was on his way to the city
of Jericho. Some robbers beat him.
They stole everything he had."

"The man was hurt. He needed help. Along came a priest. The priest saw the man, but he did not stop. Along came a helper in the temple. He saw the man but did not stop. Along came a Samaritan man. When he saw the hurt man, he stopped. The Samaritan man cleaned up the man's wounds."

"He lifted the man onto his own donkey and took him down the road to an inn. They stayed at the inn. The Samaritan man took care of the hurt man all night long," said Jesus.

"In the morning, the Samaritan man gave
the innkeeper two silver coins and said,
'Take good care of him until I return.'"

After Jesus finished the story, he asked,
"Which one of the three men was the
neighbor?" The lawyer answered,
"The one who took care of the hurt man."
Jesus said, "Go and do as he did."

Mary and Martha

Luke 10:38–42

Mary, Martha, and their brother
Lazarus were friends with Jesus.

125

One day Jesus came over to visit.
Mary sat at his feet and listened
to him for a long time.

Meanwhile, Martha was busy cooking
and cleaning. There was so much to do!

The longer Mary listened to Jesus,
the madder Martha got. She said,
"I am busy in the kitchen while
Mary is doing nothing!"

"Jesus, please tell my sister to help me,"
Martha whined.

"Martha, Martha," said Jesus,
"You should not be upset.
Mary has chosen what is better.
She is listening to me."

The Lost Sheep

Matthew 18:10–14; Luke 15:3–7

Some people wondered who was most important to God. So Jesus told them a parable.

"Think about a shepherd. What does
he do? He watches over his sheep.
He gives them plenty of food, and
he gives them plenty of water."

132

"He counts them up to make sure
they are all there. If one is lost,
he looks for it. He looks in the barn.
He looks near the stream. He looks
in the hills. He looks everywhere."

"The shepherd does not give up.
At last, he finds the little lost sheep!"

"He carries the sheep back.
He calls his friends together
and says, 'Let's celebrate!
My lost sheep has been found!'"

Then Jesus said, "God loves every one of his children like a shepherd loves his sheep. When one of them sins, it is like a sheep that has gone astray, and God is very sad. But when the person turns away from sin and comes back to God, he is very, very happy. He celebrates like a shepherd who has found his lost sheep."

The Lost Son

Luke 15:11–32

Jesus told another parable about God's love. "There was a man who had two sons," said Jesus. "He owned a big farm."

137

"His youngest son did not want to
work anymore. He wanted to travel
and have fun. So he asked his father
for his share of the family money."

"The son got the money. He packed his
things and left. He couldn't wait to see the
world! His family was sad to see him go."

"At first he had fun spending the money.
He bought expensive clothes,
and he ate fancy food.
But soon all the money was gone."

"He had to go to work and he got a job
with a pig farmer. He was so hungry
that even the pigs' food looked good.
The son wanted to go back home.
He said, 'I will tell my father
I am sorry for what I have done.
I do not deserve to be called his son.
Maybe he will let me work for him.'"

141

"The father saw his son coming
down the road. His eyes filled
with tears as he ran to greet him."

"The son said, 'Please forgive me, Dad.'
That night, they had a big party.
The father exclaimed, 'My son
was lost, but now he's found.'"

Jesus explained his story.
"God is like this father. He is full
of love and joy when people who
are lost come back to him."

Ten Lepers

Luke 17:11–19

As Jesus was traveling, he met ten *lepers*.
Their bodies were covered with sores.
The lepers shouted,
"Jesus, please heal us!"

Jesus said, "Go. Show yourselves
to the priests." The ten lepers left.
While they were walking away,
something amazing happened.

All ten of them were healed! Only
one man went back to thank Jesus.

He threw himself at Jesus' feet
and said, "Thank you!"
Jesus wondered where the other
men were. They did not come
back to thank him.

Jesus and the Children

Matthew 19:13–15; Mark 10:13–16; Luke 18:15–17

The children loved to spend time
with Jesus.

But the disciples didn't understand.
They said, "Stop. Do not bother Jesus.
He is just too busy."

Jesus told the disciples, "Let the children
come to me. Do not keep them away.
You must become like these little children
if you want to enter God's kingdom."

Then Jesus blessed the children.

A Short Man

Luke 19:1–10

People crowded the streets to see Jesus.
Zacchaeus wanted to see, too,
but he was too short.
So he climbed up a tree.

153

As Jesus was passing by, he looked up
and said, "Zacchaeus, come down.
I want to go to your house."
Zacchaeus scrambled down the tree.

Zaccheus was a tax collector. His job
was to get the tax money from the people
and give it to the king. Nobody liked him.
He was surprised but happy that Jesus
wanted to come to *his* house!

A crowd of people stood outside
the house. They grumbled,
"Why is Jesus in *there*?"

Zacchaeus told Jesus, "I will give money
to the poor. And I will pay back anyone
I have cheated. In fact, I will give them
back more money than I took."
Jesus was happy that Zacchaeus
was going to make things right.

Lazarus Lives Again

John 11:1–44

One day, Jesus received a message
from Mary and Martha.
"Jesus, please come quickly.
Lazarus is very sick." But Jesus stayed
where he was for two more days.

Then Jesus traveled to the place
where Mary and Martha lived.
Martha went to meet him.
She was crying.

Martha said to Jesus, "My dear brother
has died. If you had been here,
you could have healed him."
Jesus was sad. He cried, too.

Then Jesus walked over to Lazarus's tomb.
He told some men to roll away the stone.
Jesus prayed out loud, "Father, I know
you always hear me. Now, show everyone
that you have sent me."

Then Jesus shouted, "Lazarus, come out!"
Lazarus walked out of the tomb. He was
alive again! Everyone was amazed.
Many people believed in Jesus that day.

A Gift for Jesus

John 12:1–8

One evening, Jesus and his disciples were
visiting Mary, Martha, and Lazarus.

Mary poured some expensive perfume on Jesus' feet. Then she dried his feet with her hair.

Judas was one of the disciples. He said,
"That perfume cost a lot of money.
Mary should have sold it and given
the money to the poor."

Jesus knew the truth—that Judas wanted
the money for himself. Jesus replied,
"Mary did what is right. She honored me.
You will always have the poor among you.
But you won't always have me here."

The True King

Matthew 21:1–11; Mark 11:1–11; Luke 19:29–42; John 12:12–19

Jesus and his disciples went to Jerusalem
for the Passover Feast. Jesus told
two disciples to bring him a donkey.
He told them where to find it.

Jesus rode the donkey to Jerusalem.

A big crowd welcomed him.

People waved palm branches and put
them on the road in front of Jesus.

They shouted, "Hosanna! Hosanna!
Blessed is the king of Israel!"

The leaders in Jerusalem did not
like Jesus. They saw how many people
were following him, and they were
angry about it. They were jealous.

A Poor Widow's Gift

Mark 12:41–44; Luke 21:1–4

Jesus and the disciples went to the temple area. They watched people drop money into the *offering* box.

The rich people put a lot of money
into the box.

Then Jesus saw a poor *widow*.
She put two small coins into the box.
"This woman's gift is greater than
all the others," Jesus whispered to
his disciples.

"Even though the woman is poor,
she gave *all* the money she had.
The rich people gave a lot of money,
but they still have plenty left over."

Washing the Disciples' Feet

John 13:3–30

Jesus and his disciples gathered together
for a special Passover meal. Jesus knew
he would be leaving them soon.

After supper, Jesus removed his outer
clothing. He wrapped a towel around
his waist. Then he filled a bowl with
water. Jesus washed and dried the
disciples' feet, one by one.

Then it was Peter's turn. He said to Jesus,
"Lord, you should never wash my feet."
Jesus answered, "I *must* wash your feet
for you to be part of my kingdom." Then
he said to them all, "As I have washed
your feet, you must wash each other's
feet." By doing this, Jesus showed his
friends how to love and serve each other.

Jesus told them, "One of you will
turn against me tonight."
His disciples were shocked and said,
"We would *never* do that!"

"Who will turn against you?" John asked.
"The one I give this piece of bread to,"
said Jesus. He handed it to Judas and said,
"Do what you must." Judas quickly left.

The Last Supper

Matthew 26:17–29; Mark 14:12–25; Luke 22:7–19; John 13–14

Then Jesus did something else.
He picked up a loaf of bread and blessed it.
Then he broke it into pieces.
He gave the bread to his disciples to eat.
Jesus said, "This bread is my body.
Every time you do this, think of me."

In the same way, he took a cup of wine
and blessed it. He gave it to the disciples
to drink. "This is my blood. It is poured
out to forgive the sins of many."

"The time has come for me to go away.
Where I am going, you cannot go yet.
I am going to *heaven* to prepare a
wonderful new home for you.
But I will return to you soon."

"At first, you will be very sad.
But do not be frightened.
Soon you will understand
and you will be filled with joy."

Jesus Is Arrested
and Crucified

Matthew 26–27; Mark 14–15; Luke 22–23; John 18–19

Judas went to the leaders. He asked,
"How much will you pay me if I help
you capture Jesus?" They said,
"Thirty pieces of silver." So Judas took
the money and made a plan.

Jesus had gone to his favorite garden
to pray. The disciples went along.
Jesus prayed, "Father, if it is your will,
I am ready to give my life so that
all the people who trust in me will be
saved from their sins."

Soon, Judas arrived with some soldiers.
Peter wanted to protect Jesus.
But Jesus said, "No. I must allow this
to happen." All the disciples ran away,
and the soldiers arrested Jesus.

They took Jesus to the leaders.
The leaders said, "You say that
you are the Son of God.
We do not believe you."

The soldiers took charge of Jesus.
They made him carry a big wooden cross.
They took him to a place called
The Skull (*Golgotha*).
There they nailed Jesus to the cross.

Jesus died on the cross.

Everyone who loved Jesus was very sad.
But they forgot something important. Jesus
had said he would see them again soon!

Jesus Is Risen!

Matthew 28:1–10; Mark 16:1–10; Luke 24:1–11; John 20:1–18

After Jesus died, some of his
friends laid his body in a big tomb.
They sealed it shut with a large round
stone. Soldiers guarded the tomb.

Three days later, the earth shook. An angel
of the LORD came down from heaven and
pushed the stone away from the tomb.
Then the angel sat on the stone.

When the soldiers saw the angel,
they fell to the ground.

Mary was walking to the tomb with
some of her friends. They saw the
angel, who said, "Do not be afraid.
Jesus is not here. He has risen!"

"Go and tell Peter and the other disciples that Jesus is alive!"

On their way, the women saw Jesus.
They fell to their knees and worshiped
him. Jesus smiled and said, "Go tell the
others that I will see them in Galilee."
So Mary ran to tell the disciples.

Jesus Returns

John 20:19–20

The disciples had locked themselves in a small room because they were afraid the leaders would send soldiers to arrest them.

199

Suddenly, Jesus appeared to them!
He said, "Peace be with you."
They thought he was a ghost. But Jesus
said, "Touch my hands and my feet
so that you will know it is really me."

The disciples cheered! They were
very, very happy to see Jesus again.

A Net Full of Fish

John 21:1–14

Peter went fishing with some of the
disciples. They fished from their
boat all night, but they did not
even catch one fish.

Early the next morning, someone from
the shore shouted, "You have not caught
any fish, have you?"
"No," they replied.
"Cast your net to the right side of the
boat," the man said.

As soon as they did, their net was
full of fish! Then Peter knew the man
was Jesus. He jumped out of the boat
and swam to shore.

Jesus asked him, "Do you love me?"
Peter said, "You know I do."
Jesus said, "If you love me, then
take good care of my people."

Jesus Goes to Heaven

Matthew 28:16–20, Luke 24:44–51; Acts 1:6–11

Jesus had told his disciples, "I gave my life
so that you could be with me in heaven.
I am going there to prepare a wonderful
new home for you. When I come back the
next time, I will take you with me."
But now it was time for Jesus to leave.

Jesus said, "God has given me
complete power over heaven and earth.
Go and tell everyone the good news.
Make new disciples. Baptize them and
teach them to obey my commandments.
Don't ever forget, I will always be
with you."

"Go to Jerusalem and wait there,"
said Jesus. "The Holy Spirit will come to
you. He will give you power to tell people
about me. Now the time has come for me
to go to heaven. Do not be afraid."

Then Jesus went up toward heaven
in a cloud. His disciples stared at the
sky for a long time.

All of a sudden, two angels appeared.
They asked, "Why are you standing here
looking at the sky? Jesus will return the
same way you saw him go."

Then the disciples remembered what Jesus
had said. They returned to Jerusalem and
waited for the Holy Spirit to come.

The Holy Spirit Comes

Acts 2

Thousands of people went to Jerusalem to celebrate a Jewish holiday called *Pentecost*. They came from many countries and spoke many different languages. Jesus' disciples were staying there. They were praying together.

Suddenly, a noise filled the room.
It sounded like a strong wind blowing.
The Holy Spirit appeared as
tongues of fire on each of them.

They started talking in languages
they did not know.
The people in Jerusalem heard the noise
and came to see what was happening.

The crowd was amazed and asked,
"How are you able to speak *our*
languages?" Peter said, "The prophets
told us this would happen."

Then Peter told them about God's plan.
"God sent Jesus to save everyone
from the bad things we have done."

The people asked, "What should we do?"
Peter replied, "Ask Jesus to forgive you
for your sins and be baptized in the
name of Jesus Christ."

On that day, 3,000 people believed in
Jesus. The disciples baptized all of them.

The First Church

Acts 2:42–47

The new believers studied with
the disciples. They learned many
things about God and God's plans.

They prayed together.

They sang songs and praised God.

They ate meals and celebrated the Lord's Supper together. They shared everything they had with each other.
God added more and more believers to the church every day.

The Lame Man

Acts 3:1–10

One day, Peter and John were going
to the temple. They saw a man
who could not walk. He had not
been able to walk his whole life.
The man was begging for money.

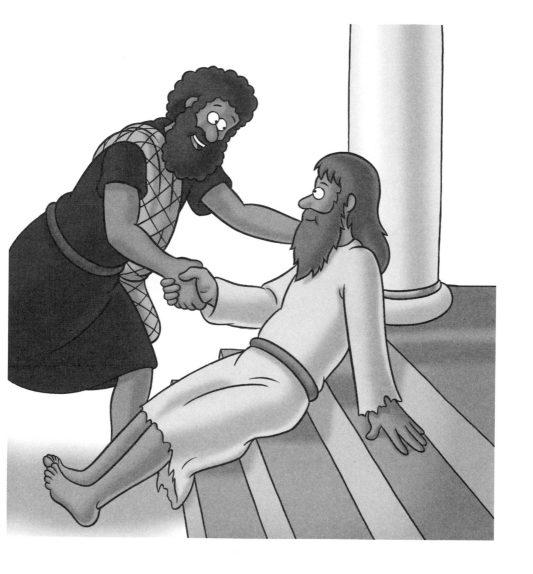

Peter told him, "We have no silver or gold.
But we will give you what we do have.
In Jesus' name, stand up and walk!"

Immediately, the man jumped up.
His legs were strong! He began
walking and leaping and praising God.

All the people who saw him were amazed.
Peter told the people, "We did not
make this man walk. Jesus did." Many
more people believed in Jesus that day.

A Changed Man

Acts 9:1–19

Saul did not like Jesus' followers. He was on his way to put some of them in jail.

Suddenly, a bright light flashed around
him. Saul fell to the ground. A loud voice
asked, "Saul, why are you against me?"
Saul was afraid. He cried out,
"Who are you?" The voice replied,
"I am Jesus, the one you are against."

"Go to Damascus and you will be told
what to do." When Saul got up, he
could not see.

Some men who were traveling
with Saul led him to the city.
Jesus had also appeared to a man named
Ananias. Jesus led Ananias to Saul.

Ananias laid his hands on Saul and said,
"Jesus sent me to you. You may see again.
Be filled with the Holy Spirit."
Immediately Saul could see!
Then Ananias baptized him.

After this, God changed Saul's name
to Paul. He was a new man! Instead of
hating Jesus' followers, he loved them.
And he became a follower, too.

Paul's Journeys

Acts 9:20–43

Paul traveled far and wide. He taught everyone he met about Jesus. The new believers were called *Christians* because they were followers of Jesus Christ.

Paul traveled with different helpers.
He shared the good news with everyone
he met. He baptized many people.

During Paul's travels,
he started many churches.

Sometimes he would walk for
miles and miles.

Paul's Missionary Journeys
← (A.D. 46-48)
← (A.D. 49-52)
← (A.D. 53-57)
← (A.D. 59-60)

Rome

Syracuse

Other times, he would take
a boat across the seas.

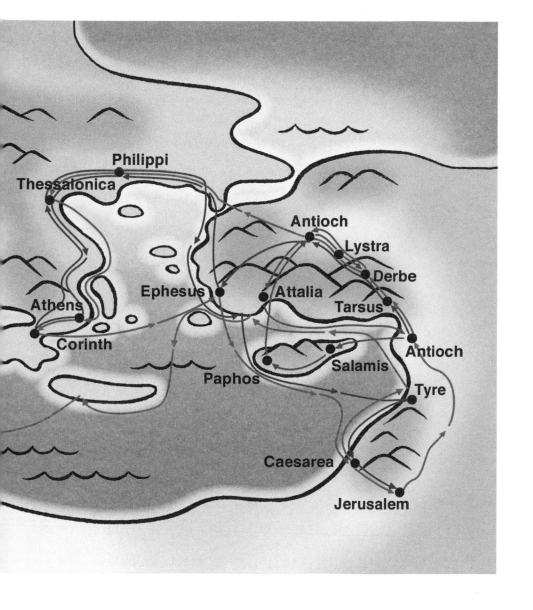

He told everyone about Jesus'
love for them.

Earthquake in Prison

Acts 16:24–34

Some people did not like Paul and his
friend Silas preaching about Jesus.
One day, they were thrown into prison.
But they were not worried. They knew
God would take care of them.

That night, God sent an earthquake.
It shook so hard that all the prison doors
opened up and all the prisoners'
chains fell off. The guard thought
everyone had escaped. He was terrified!

241

Paul told the guard, "Do not worry.
We are still here." The guard was amazed.
He invited the two men to his house.

The guard and his family learned
about Jesus and decided to follow him.
The next day, Paul and Silas left
to tell more people about Jesus.

Jesus Is Coming!

Revelation 1:1–2; 21:2–4

Many years later, the disciple John lived on an island. While he was there, an angel came to him in a *vision*.

In the vision, a bright light surrounded
Jesus. He spoke to John, "Do not be
afraid. Write a book about what you
see and send it to the churches."

In the vision, John saw God sitting on his throne. A rainbow sparkled all around him. John saw that everything bad on the earth had come to an end.

Then John saw a new heaven and a
new earth. God said, "There will be
no more death or sadness or crying or
pain. I will live with my people forever."

Then Jesus promised,
"I am coming back soon."

The Beginner's Bible
DICTIONARY

Some of the words in this book may be new to you. Throughout the stories you will see these words in italics. You can find out what they mean by using this dictionary.

Angel: A spirit who is God's helper. A spirit who tells people God's words.

Amen: A Hebrew word that means "so be it" or "let it become true."

Baptize: To sprinkle, pour on, or cover a person with water. It is a sign that the person belongs to Jesus.

Christians: People who believe Jesus has forgiven their sins and will someday live with him forever in heaven.

Disciple: A person who follows a teacher. This person does what their teacher says to do.

Faith: Trust and belief in God. Knowing God is real, even though we can't see him.

Heaven: 1. The place where God lives. 2. The sky. 3. Where Christians go after they die.

Holy Spirit: God's Spirit who creates life. He helps people do God's work. He helps people to believe in Jesus, to love him and to live like him.

Kingdom: An area or group of people ruled by a king.

Leprosy: A word used in the bible for many different skin diseases and infections. People with leprosy, called lepers, during Bible times had to live in separate communities so they wouldn't infect others.

Manger: A food box for animals.

Miracle: An amazing thing that happens that only God can do. This includes such things as calming a storm or bringing someone back to life.

Offering: Something people give to God. It was and is a part of their worship.

Parable: A story that Jesus told to teach people.

Passover: A feast that was celebrated every year to remember the time when God set the people of Israel free from Egypt. God "passed over" their homes if they were marked with blood in the doorways.

Pentecost: 1. A Jewish celebration held 50 days after Passover. 2. The day the Holy Spirit came in a special way to live in Christians.

Savior: The One who saves us from our sins. A name belonging to Jesus Christ.

Temple: The building where the Jewish people worshiped God and brought their sacrifices. God was present there in a special way.

Widow: A woman whose husband has died.

Vision: A dream from God. The person who saw it was usually awake. God gave these kinds of dreams to people to show them what he was going to do.

If you enjoyed the New Testament, you'll love the full Bible.

Hardcover • 6 ¼" x 7 ½" • ISBN 0-310-70962-8

The bestselling Bible storybook of our time—over 5 million sold!

Introduce children to the stories and characters of the Bible with this best-loved Bible storybook. Now updated with vibrant new art, text, and stories, more than 90 favorite Bible stories come to life, making *The Beginner's Bible*® the perfect starting point for children. They will enjoy the fun illustrations of Noah helping the elephant onto the ark, Jonah praying inside the fish, and more as they discover *The Beginner's Bible*® just like millions of children before.

Available at your local bookstore!

The Beginner's Bible for Toddlers®
Hardcover • 9780310714088

This condensed version of the full-size *The Beginner's Bible*® will serve as an introduction to well-known Bible stories—perfect for toddlers just starting to learn about the Bible.

Available at your local bookstore!

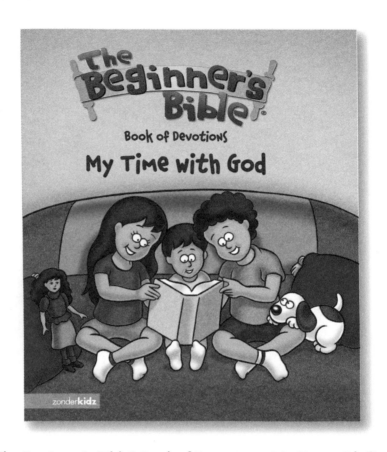

The Beginner's Bible® Book of Devotions—My Time with God
Hardcover • 9780310714811

Filled with vibrant, fresh Beginner's Bible® artwork, this devotional is filled with a year's worth of readings that will help preschoolers learn the themes from basic Bible stories and apply them to their lives, through prayers, songs, and fun activities.

Available at your local bookstore!

Adam and Eve in the Garden
Softcover • 9780310715528

Daniel and the Lions
Softcover • 9780310715511

David and the Giant
Softcover • 9780310715504

Esther and the King
Softcover• 9780310714606

Jesus and His Friends
Softcover• 9780310714613

Jesus Saves the World
Softcover• 9780310715535

Jonah and the Big Fish
Softcover• 9780310714590

Noah and the Ark
Softcover• 9780310714583

Available at your local bookstore!

The Beginner's Bible® brand has sold more than 14 million worldwide since 1989 and continues to be a favorite for children and parents.

To learn more about The Beginner's Bible® products, please write to us at:

5300 Patterson Avenue, S.E.
Grand Rapids, MI 49530